THE BERLIN AIRLIFT

THE BERLIN AIRLIFT

Scott Westerfeld

Silver Burdett Press, Inc.
Englewood Cliffs, New Jersey

Acknowledgments
The author thanks Jacqueline Ogburn for her invaluable assistance in reviewing and editing the manuscript.

Consultants:
We thank the following people for reviewing the manuscript and offering their helpful suggestions:

Michael Kort
Associate Professor of Social Science
Boston University

Richard M. Haynes
Assistant Professor
Division of Administration, Curriculum and Instruction
Director of the Office of Field Experiences and Teacher Placement
School of Education and Psychology
Western Carolina University

Contents page photo courtesy of Wide World Photos.
Title page photo courtesy of the George C. Marshall Library.
Cover photo courtesy of the Hoover Institute, German Pictorial Collection.

Library of Congress Cataloging-in-Publication Data

Westerfeld, Scott.
    The Berlin airlift / by Scott Westerfeld.
        p.   cm.—(Turning points in American history)
    Bibliography: p.
    Includes index.
    1. Berlin (Germany) History—Blockade, 1948-1949—Juvenile
literature. I. Title. II. Series.
    DD881.W473   1989   89-6173
    943.1'550874—dc20   CIP
        ISBN 0-382-09852-8 (pbk.) ISBN 0-382-09833-1   AC
    (lib. bdg.)

Editorial coordination by Richard G. Gallin

 Created by Media Projects Incorporated

C. Carter Smith, *Executive Editor*
Toni Rachiele, *Managing Editor*
Charles Wills, *Project Editor*
Bernard Schleifer, *Design Consultant*
Simon Hu, *Cartographer*

ISBN 0-382-09833-1 [lib. bdg.]
10 9 8 7 6 5 4 3 2 1

ISBN 0-382-09852-8 [pbk.]
10 9 8 7 6 5 4 3 2 1

CONTENTS

INTRODUCTION

AN ISLAND OF DARKNESS

Night was falling on Berlin.

The dark outlines of broken buildings loomed over the city streets. In the distance, the rumble of a Soviet tank could be heard. It was June 24, 1948, and the German capital lay in ruins.

Three years before, American bombs and Soviet artillery had reduced Berlin to a pile of rubble. Then, Soviet troops had stormed Hitler's capital, and the Nazi banner had been lowered forever. In its place flew the flags of the United Kingdom, the Soviet Union, France, and the United States. Berlin had been divided among the four powers, whose combined efforts had destroyed Hitler's Germany. Together they hoped to forge a new and peaceful Europe.

But now the victors were struggling among themselves. Between Moscow and Washington, a dangerous contest was taking place, and the fate of the shattered city rested on the outcome.

As night fell, the western half of the city slipped into utter darkness. The Allied sector—administered by the French, British, and Americans—was deep inside Soviet-occupied territory. The Soviets had severed the rail and road links that connected western Berlin with Allied territory. For six days the only route into or out of the city had been by air.

Today the electricity, supplied by generators in the Soviet-controlled sector of Berlin, had been cut off.

As darkness covered the western sector, its 2 million inhabitants wondered where the food, water, and power necessary for their survival would come from. The Soviet Union wanted the West out of the city and was willing to strangle Berlin slowly to force the West out. The Americans and British had sacrificed much to destroy Berlin and all it represented. Would they now risk war to save it?

A worker puts a "Made in Blockaded Berlin" label on a crate. The bear, symbol of Berlin, is shown in chains.

A German volunteer crew unloads flour from the cargo hold of a C-47. The aircraft, also called the "Globemaster," could carry twenty tons of flour in one load.

There were 6,000 troops in the Allied garrison. In the countryside around the darkened city were half a million Russian soldiers.

The only hopeful sound that night came from the aircraft landing at Berlin's Templehof airport. General Lucius Clay, the commander-in-chief of U.S.-occupied Germany, had begun an air supply operation on his own authority. Some food was getting in, but 2 million people could not be fed by airlift. How long would the Soviets keep their stranglehold on the city?

The precarious situation of western Berlin in 1948 had its origins in the tumult of World War II. In that massive confrontation, countries perished and new countries were formed, the United Nations was created, and the map of Europe was forever altered. After the smoke cleared, Berlin, former capital of Nazi Germany, emerged as the lone outpost of democracy in Soviet-occupied Europe. It was here that the Soviet Union and the United States began their global struggle. Around this strange "island," forces were gathering that could plunge the world into another war.

Night fell, and save for the runway lights at Templehof airport, the darkness was complete.

1

EUROPE IN RUINS

On August 21, 1939, an announcement was made in Berlin that astonished the world. In complete secrecy, the governments of Nazi Germany and the Soviet Union had concluded negotiations on a fateful treaty. Called a "nonaggression pact," it bound both nations to remain at peace with each other for ten years. The two architects of the treaty were Adolf Hitler and Joseph Stalin, the dictators of two great, and feared, European powers.

Hitler had ruled Germany for six years. As a corporal in World War I, he had witnessed Germany's defeat and humiliation at the hands of the victorious Allies. After the war, Germany was forced to pay huge sums to the Allies as war reparations. The borders of Europe had been redrawn by the victors. Germany was made smaller and

This painting of the ruined city of Caen, in Normandy, France, depicts the destruction Europe suffered in World War II.

split in two by a corridor of Poland. The Allies—France, Britain, and the United States—thought that a weakened Germany would be less of a threat to future peace. The war reparations shattered the German economy and made the peace a bitter one for the German people.

Hitler climbed to power in the wreckage of this defeated country. He used the harsh terms forced upon Germany after the war to fuel the anger of proud Germans. Hitler's political party, the National Socialists, or Nazis, became the largest in Germany. They promised to end payment of war reparations and to restore Germany as a major European power. Although the Nazis had not yet received a majority of votes, Hitler was appointed chancellor.

The Nazis soon did away with political freedoms guaranteed by the German constitution. The other political parties, especially the Socialists and Communists, were harassed and their leadership imprisoned. At the next election there was little opposition left, and the Nazis received 92 percent of the vote.

In other countries where the economy had faltered, disillusioned people were giving their loyalty to leaders like Hitler. This movement toward strong, totalitarian rulers was called fascism. Fascists like Benito Mussolini in Italy took advantage of people's dissatisfaction and bigotry, which were heightened by the depression sweeping through Europe, and they used fear of communism as an excuse to persecute their political enemies.

Under Nazi rule the anger of the German people was directed against France and Britain, against the smaller neighboring countries that had been carved out of Germany after World War I, and, most viciously, against the Jews. Through threats, violence, and coercion, the Nazis gained complete power and succeeded in reviving the German economy. They also rebuilt the German military machine, which became the most modern in the world.

In the late 1930s Hitler felt the time was ripe for Germany to set upon a program of conquest. He pressured the democracies of Europe into concession after concession. They tried to appease him, thinking that meeting his demands would preserve the peace. One by one, the Rhineland, Austria, and Czechoslovakia came under German military control. Finally, France and Britain drew the line at Poland.

Hitler wanted Poland, however. It was the country that separated the two halves of Germany. He knew by invading Poland, he might provoke a war with France and Britain, so, he moved to protect his back. Hitler believed he could defeat the Western powers if the Soviet Union remained neutral. With this in mind, he sent Nazi Foreign Minister Joachim von Ribbentrop to Moscow, with an offer of peace to his hated enemy, Joseph Stalin.

Stalin had taken over the leadership of the young Union of Soviet Socialist Republics after Vladimir Lenin's death in 1924. Since the revolution of 1917, which had brought the Communists to power, Russia had been ostracized from most of the European community of nations. From 1917 to 1920 a fierce civil war raged between the Communist Bolsheviks (the "Reds") and the anti-Communist forces ("Whites"). Fearing the emergence of a communist power in Europe, many countries—including the United States, France, and Britain—sent troops to aid the "Whites." After Communist victory, their leaders were filled with suspicion and hatred for the outside world.

When Stalin came to power, he increased the already tight control the Soviet government held over life in the U.S.S.R. He drove out fellow revolutionary Leon Trotsky, who had led the Soviet army in the civil war and later had him assassinated in Mexican exile. As the sole power in the U.S.S.R., Stalin became ever more brutal and paranoid. Under his rule, several million people in the Ukraine died from starvation during the forced collectivization of farming.

American soldiers in Archangel, Russia, in 1919, using reindeer to travel over frozen rivers. They were sent to fight against the newly formed Communist government of the Soviet Union, but were withdrawn in 1920.

This was known as the Terror Famine. In the 1930s he began a series of rigged trials to eliminate those who had displeased him. Stalin called them "betrayers of the revolution." Several million people, including hundreds of thousands of loyal Communists, were executed, jailed, or sent to Siberia. These "purges" continued for years.

Stalin's motivations for signing the fateful treaty are still unclear. Perhaps Stalin, like Hitler, sought revenge against the West. Possibly, he hoped that Hitler's war of conquest would leave the Soviet Union untouched, and that communism would rule Europe after democracy and fascism had destroyed each other. Stalin was also about to invade Finland and, like Hitler, needed to be sure that Germany and the Soviet Union would not go to war. Whatever his reasons, the pact sealed Poland's fate. Since Hitler's eastern border was safe, he could begin his war with France and Britain. Stalin had also sealed the fate of Europe. For the next six years, the world would be plunged into the most destructive war in history.

Only nine days after the "non-aggression pact" was signed, German troops swept into Poland. France and Britain, as they had threatened, declared war against Germany. Sixteen days later, by a secret provision of the pact, Soviet troops invaded eastern Poland. The sight of the two dictatorships carving up a small nation dismayed the world. World War II had begun.

Poland, attacked from two sides, lasted barely a month. Thanks to his pact with the Soviet Union, Hitler was able to leave only token forces in Poland and turn his full energies toward France.

The leadership of France thought that the war would be fought as World War I had been. Behind their heavily fortified border with Germany, the French assumed they could hold back the Nazis until Great Britain or the United States delivered aid. The war in Poland revealed a different story. German tanks, mechanized infantry, and air power had shown how quickly a war could be won. This was a new form of mechanical war, called "blitzkrieg," or "lightning war."

After a period of inactivity, called the "phony war," the blitzkrieg struck westward. The German army invaded neutral Belgium and the Netherlands on May 10, 1940, bombing the two small countries mercilessly. Parachute and glider troops landed throughout the countryside. The Dutch attempted to stop the German advance by opening dikes and flooding much of their country. That very day, British Prime Minister Neville Chamberlain, who had worked so hard to appease Hitler, resigned, and Winston Churchill became prime minister. He was to lead his country through more than five years of war.

The German army crossed over the Belgian border with France on May 14. Thousands of citizens fled from Paris at the news, and Premier Paul Reynaud of France told Churchill, "We are beaten!" Italy's Mussolini decided to join Hitler, attacking France from the south. Within five weeks the French had surrendered.

The blitzkrieg had swept through France so quickly that the country had sustained little damage. Paris was virtually untouched. It would not be so for England.

The English Channel protected Great Britain from a land invasion, and the Germans knew they could not defeat the British navy. The Battle of Britain was fought in the air. Night after night, thousands of German bombers filled the English sky. London, the capital, suffered the worst bombing. Families were split as children were taken to the countryside. The air raids killed forty thousand civilians and destroyed one million homes from September 1940 to May 1941. Modern warfare had entered a new era of destructiveness.

But the costs were heavy for the German air force. The British had developed radar shortly before the war, and the Royal Air Force fighter planes were always waiting for the cumbersome German bombers. The British people, instead of calling on their leaders to surrender, simply became more determined. Realizing that the British would not submit, Hitler called off the attacks. The German war machine in the West finally stopped.

Hitler turned his military might eastward again. With his "ten-year" treaty with Stalin only two years old, he invaded the U.S.S.R. in June 1941. It proved to be one of his worst mistakes.

The blitzkrieg swept forward as it had in France. German troops reached the gates of Moscow in nine weeks. The Soviet Union was a far larger country than France, however, and the Germans were slowed by the distance their supplies had to travel. The strategy that hurt them the most was Stalin's "scorched earth" policy. He declared that nothing would be left for the advancing Germans. Crops were burned, villages destroyed, and oil reserves emptied. The Germans advanced into a vast wasteland, and as the harsh Russian winter began to fall, the Soviets rallied and counterattacked. The Germans suffered a disastrous defeat at Stalingrad, in the fall and winter of 1942–1943. After that winter, which caught them ill prepared, the Germans began a slow retreat on all fronts.

While these battles raged, Germany continued its policy of sending millions of people from the conquered countries to Germany to work as slave laborers. Hundreds of thousands were worked to death in German war factories. Millions were thrown into concentration camps. In special death camps and other organized places of murder, the Nazis systematically killed six million Jews, most of them citizens of Poland and the Soviet Union.

The United States entered the war after the Japanese attack on Pearl Harbor, in December 1941. (In 1940 Japan, Germany, and Italy had become a triple alliance, and were called the Axis Powers.) By 1943 twenty-six nations were at war with the Axis. These twenty-six countries agreed to cooperate during the war and when peace came would be the core of the United Nations.

Finally, the destructive force of air power was turned back upon Germany. With the great industrial might of the United States behind the attacks, they far exceeded what Germany had done to Britain. In a single week of raids on Hamburg, more civilians died than in the entire Battle of Britain. City after city

In Pirmasens, Germany, the Allied bombings left few buildings standing.

was engulfed in flames. Millions were left homeless.

On the Eastern Front, the Soviet army began pushing the Germans back. In June 1944 the Western Allies invaded Normandy, in France. Hitler now had what he feared most: a two-front war. As the Germans retreated, they destroyed railroads, villages, and supplies, creating a "scorched earth" of their own.

By 1945 the Allies were assured of victory. In early February, Franklin Roosevelt, Winston Churchill, and Joseph Stalin met in Yalta to discuss the shape of Europe after the war. The "Big Three," as they were called, divided Germany into four zones. The Soviets, British, French, and Americans were each to administer one zone. Roosevelt, in his fourth term of office and stricken with disease, gave Stalin a free hand in Eastern Europe and guaranteed the Soviets would be paid war reparations from the Western zones of Germany. In exchange, the Soviet Union would go to war with Japan after Germany's fall. Stalin also promised Poland a representative government, and eventually, free elections, provided that the new government of Poland would be "friendly" to the Soviet Union.

At that time there were two Polish governments. One was the London government, which had been in power before the war and had fled to England as Poland fell. They had watched the Soviet invasion of eastern Poland with horror and had little love for Stalin. Then, when German forces had first swept toward the Soviet Union, the world had discovered an awful secret. In a mass grave at Katyn, Poland, fourteen thousand corpses were buried—an entire generation of Polish officer cadets whom the Soviets had captured and put to death. When news of the Katyn massacre reached London, the Polish government in exile was outraged and demanded an explanation from the Soviets. Stalin claimed it was a German trick and angrily cut off relations with the London Poles. When Soviet troops took Poland back from Germany, they formed their own government, whose capital was in Lublin, made up of Communist partisans who were friendly to Stalin. One of the agreements reached at Yalta was that both these governments would be represented after the war.

It was over the invasion of Poland that France and Britain had gone to war, and the Western Allies wanted to guarantee Polish freedom after all the sacrifices they had made. What remained to be seen was whether Stalin would keep his promises.

Poland was only one of the many problems facing the victors as the war ground to a halt. The toll that six years of struggle had taken on Europe was tremendous. London still smoldered from Nazi bombs and from the German "revenge" weapons, the V-1 and V-2 flying bombs, that had appeared late in the war. England had expended £30 billion in the war (the same as about $480 billion in 1980), most of which was borrowed. France had been occupied by

The "Big Three"—Stalin, Roosevelt, and Churchill—meet at Yalta in February 1945 to discuss post-war Europe.

the Germans for five years, and its society and government were filled with Nazi collaborators. One million Western Allied troops, 5 million Germans, and 20 million Russians had been killed. Hitler's concentration camps had left fewer than half the Jews of Europe alive.

The destruction of the war exceeded simply the human casualties. The very fabric of European society was in tatters. Millions were without home or country. These unfortunate survivors were called Displaced Persons, or simply DPs. Many were moved from one DP camp to another, as the victors redrew the map of Europe again. They were Germans pushed westward by the advancing Soviets, who wanted the new Poland free of German influence. They were Jews who had escaped death in the camps, only to return to homes shattered by Allied bombs and to memories of communities that had simply vanished. They were citizens of the small nations and territories that Germany and the Soviet Union had annexed, whose countries had lost their independence.

As the Allied forces drew in a tightening circle around Berlin, Churchill realized that the fate of the dispossessed of Europe rested upon whose armies controlled the remnants of Hitler's empire. Churchill appealed to General Dwight Eisenhower, supreme commander of the Western Allied armies, to make an all-out push to capture Berlin before the Soviets did. Eisenhower did not approve of mixing politics with strategy, however, and preferred to save lives with a cautious advance.

The U.S. and Soviet armies met for the first time at the Elbe River, in Germany. The Americans knew of the So-

American officers are treated to a party by the Soviet army. Behind the dancers, portraits of Stalin and the recently deceased Franklin D. Roosevelt hang side by side.

viets' hardships and were happy to meet the people who had borne the brunt of Hitler's armies for so long. For a brief time, the relationship between the two victors seemed to be a productive one. With Britain exhausted and France recovering from German occupation, it was the United States and the U.S.S.R. that would have to piece the continent of Europe together again.

Finally, the war in Europe ended. Hitler shot himself in his bunker, and the Soviets stormed Berlin and occupied Germany for sixty miles beyond the capital. Germany surrendered on May 8, 1945. Stalin agreed to split Berlin with the Western Allies, hoping that together the four victors (France was now included) could create a new, peaceful Germany.

The Allies decided to rule on the principle of agreement. None would take action in their part of Germany without the consent of the others. For the world, a new organization called the United Nations would operate on the same principle. The five permanent members of the Security Council all had to agree on any action. Britain, France, China, the United States, and the U.S.S.R. each had the power to veto resolutions. It was hoped that now, after all the destruction the war had caused, the world could be ruled by cooperation rather than conflict.

The truth was that Europe had been severed in two. Just as Berlin was partitioned between the victors, Europe was divided between East and West, between Soviet and American influence, and between communism and democracy. Soon, a new conflict was brewing in the aftermath of the war.

This new conflict would not be fought with bombers or soldiers. Nuclear weapons had made all-out war too dangerous. The new war was a cold war, fought with words, nerves, and the grim threat of atomic destruction. With the end of the old power struggles of Europe, the stage for this new kind of war was set.

It was in the divided city of Berlin, in the heart of shattered Europe, that the first "battle" of the cold war began.

President Truman addresses the charter session of the United Nations in San Francisco, April 1945.

2

THE IRON CURTAIN AND THE MARSHALL PLAN

On July 17, 1945, the Big Three met for the last time. They convened in Potsdam, a suburb of Berlin that had been spared the destruction of the Allied bombing offensive. Of the original Big Three leaders, only Stalin remained. Two months before, on April 12, President Roosevelt had suffered a fatal stroke at his Warm Springs, Georgia, retreat. Harry S. Truman, a little-known politician from Missouri who had become Roosevelt's vice-president, was now president of the United States. A few days into the conference, Truman toured the rubble-strewn city of Berlin and saw at first hand the destruction of the war and the plight of homeless, hungry Berliners. The fate of these Berliners and millions of other Europeans rested on the outcome of the Potsdam conference.

The new "Big Three"—Attlee, Truman, and Stalin—meet at the Potsdam conference in July 1945.

Winston Churchill was defeated in Britain's general election only a few days into the conference. He was replaced as prime minister by Clement Attlee, who had been his deputy throughout the war. Attlee took Churchill's place representing Britain at Potsdam.

Stalin did not trust Attlee, and Truman was not yet comfortable with his role as leading statesman of the free world. The respect that the original Big Three had developed for one another was missing. Because the war against Germany was over, the conference did not have the urgency of Yalta. Although the problems facing the Allies were as great as they had been during the war, the delegates were unable to agree on many important issues.

They drafted peace treaties with Germany's small allies but did not officially approve them. The delegates resolved that Japan's surrender should be unconditional. The Big Three concluded that

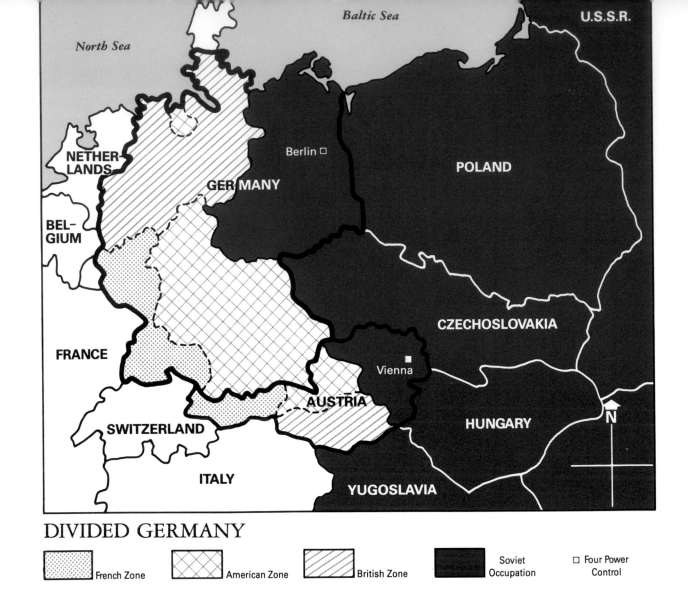

DIVIDED GERMANY

French Zone   American Zone   British Zone   Soviet Occupation   □ Four Power Control

Germany should be disarmed, and that any people associated with the Nazi party should be banned from government service. The Soviet-occupied countries of Hungary, Poland, and Czechoslovakia were to have 6 1/2 million Germans transferred from them back to Germany. A council of foreign ministers was formed to negotiate, eventually, a treaty with a new German government. There was no German government as yet, however, so the nature of the final peace agreement with Germany was left undecided.

The Western Allies remembered the lessons of the previous world war and wanted the German economy to remain intact and self-sufficient. The Soviet Union, having suffered the greatest damage in the war, demanded huge payments of raw materials and manufacturing equipment from Germany. Since all the Allied nations feared a reborn, aggressive Germany, the conference set limits on German industry and promised the Soviets payments from any extra production. The exact amount of these payments was never decided.

This lack of agreement among the victors was the first sign that a divided Europe was taking form around a divided Germany. Without specific agreements, Soviet forces were able to do what they wanted in the areas they occupied. In eastern Germany, whole factories were taken apart and shipped by train to the Soviet Union, as well as steel and raw materials. Manufactured goods were also exported without payment, in violation of the Potsdam agreements.

Meanwhile, the Allies were having trouble feeding the population of their areas. Denied grain from the Soviet zone, Britain, the United States, and France had to import food to the western zones at their own expense.

As the Soviet Union was demolishing much of Germany, it moved to increase its political control of Eastern Europe. In the countries that Soviet forces had liberated from German occupation, communist parties were assisted by the new authorities. The Soviets felt they had the right to assert pressure in whatever territories their army had occupied. In Bulgaria and Romania, the Soviets simply installed Communist governments. It was difficult for the West to protest, since these countries had been minor allies of Nazi Germany. In Yugoslavia and Albania, Communists who resisted Nazi control (called partisans) had fought off Hitler at the end of the war. They established Communist governments with little Soviet help, and Stalin's attempts to control them were not completely successful.

Soon the brutal tactics of the Soviets

were felt in Poland. At first, the government was composed of representatives from the London government, the Soviet-sponsored government, and Polish resistance groups. Stalin had promised free elections for Poland at the Yalta conference. He had been promised a "friendly" Polish government in return. Neither promise could be kept, however, because of Soviet abuses in Poland. Stalin's invasion of Poland and the massacre at Katyn were fresh in the memory of many Poles. Tensions mounted at the war's end when the Soviet Union demanded territory from the east of Poland to add to the Soviet Union. They offered German territory on Poland's western border in exchange. The London Poles and the other non-Communists rejected this proposal. The Soviets became alarmed at what they saw as an "unfriendly" rejection of their terms. The leadership of the non-Communists were threatened and thrown in jail. Soon, all those who opposed Soviet policy were imprisoned, exiled, or in hiding. The United States and Great Britain could only protest. Poland was as far from their reach as it had been when Hitler's armies had first invaded.

Only in Czechoslovakia and Finland were the Soviets true to their promise. After free elections, the Communist Party was included in these two governments, and for the moment they were spared Stalin's heavy hand.

Although the actions of the Soviet Union in Eastern Europe frustrated and alarmed the American leadership, the

Winston Churchill delivers the commencement address at Westminster College, in Missouri.

American people had other concerns. For a year, troops had been returning home and business was booming. Americans were glad to return to normal life after the long war and were not interested in the problems of Europe.

A speech made at Westminster College in Fulton, Missouri, on March 5, 1946, brought American attention back to Europe. Former prime minister Winston Churchill had been asked to speak. President Truman made a special journey from Washington for the event. Churchill told the audience of Soviet abuses and described the growing division between Eastern and Western Europe. He said, "A shadow has fallen upon the scenes so lately lighted by the Allied victory. Nobody knows what Soviet Russia and its Communist international organization intends to do in the immediate future, or what are the limits, if any, to their expansive and proselytising tendencies. . . . From Stettin in the Baltic to Trieste in the Adriatic, an iron curtain has descended across the Continent. Behind that line lie all the capitals of the ancient states of Central and Eastern Europe. Warsaw, Berlin, Prague, Vienna, Budapest, Belgrade, Bucharest, and Sofia, all these famous cities and the populations around them lie in what I must call the Soviet sphere, and all are subject in one form or another, not only to Soviet influence but to a very high and, in many cases, increasing measure of control from Moscow. . . . Whatever conclusions may be drawn from these facts—and facts they are—this is certainly not the Liberated Europe we fought to build up. Nor is it one which contains the essentials of permanent peace." The speech was widely reported, and Stalin sent Truman an angry letter demanding an apology. Truman offered Stalin free passage to speak at Fulton himself. The proposal was met with stony silence.

The wartime friendship between the Allies had been replaced by suspicion and distrust. In Europe cooperation had ended, and each occupying power did what it wanted in its own territory. In May 1946 General Lucius Clay, military governor of the American zone, angry that the Soviets were making off with the equipment that Germany needed to rebuild, stopped the payment of war reparations from American territory to the Soviet Union.

In this climate of growing division in Europe, the United States was forced to make an important decision. On February 21, 1947, an extraordinary letter from the British government was hand-delivered to the U.S. State Department. It explained that the British were no longer able to meet their commitments in the Balkans and stated bluntly that the United States would have to supply the necessary money to keep the nations of Greece and Turkey afloat.

Since the war, the government of Greece had been supported by Britain. The Communist partisans who had fought Hitler bravely during the war had been ejected from this government by the British army. Angered, the Communists returned to the guerrilla tactics they had used against the Germans, and a destructive civil war began. British aid was essential in keeping the country from falling into chaos. By 1947 the exhausted British did not have enough money to continue their support.

In Turkey, the Soviets wanted to share control of the strategically important Dardanelles strait, and to base naval and ground forces on Turkish soil. Turkey was being intimidated by Soviet armies on the Turkish-Russian border and also needed help the British could no longer afford. Great Britain was serving notice to Truman that the United States must now step in.

Truman acted immediately. In an address to Congress announcing his decision to assist Greece and Turkey, Truman declared, "I believe that it must be the policy of the United States to support free peoples who are resisting outside pressures." In committing the United States to help threatened nations anywhere on the globe, Truman moved the entire world into a new phase of international relations. This policy became known as the "Truman Doctrine," and set the stage for a worldwide confrontation with the U.S.S.R.

For two years after the war, the United States had hesitated, unsure of its position in the postwar world. Now

President Truman signs the Foreign Assistance Act, committing American aid to Greece and Turkey.

HARRY S. TRUMAN LIBRARY

GEORGE CATLETT MARSHALL (1880–1959)

George Catlett Marshall was a soldier for half a century, and he was the highest-ranking officer in the United States military during the bloodiest war in history. It is for his contributions to the cause of peace, however, that he is best remembered. His influence on American policy in the crucial years after World War II made him one of the most important statesmen of the modern era.

Marshall was born in Uniontown, Pennsylvania. He graduated from the Virginia Military Institute in 1901 and joined the army. After serving in the Philippines, he attended the Command and General Staff School, and held important staff positions during World War I. Between the world wars he was an aide to General John J. Pershing. He also served in China for three years and held a number of positions as a military educator. He was the senior instructor for the Illinois National Guard when chosen to be the Army Chief of Staff in 1939.

As President Franklin D. Roosevelt's highest military officer during World War II, he understood the extent of the wartime destruction in Europe. He made a point of supplying the president with casualty reports each week, so that Roosevelt would not lose sight of the individual soldiers whose lives were being lost. After Roosevelt's death in 1945, he held important positions under President Harry S. Truman. Truman, inexperienced in foreign affairs, relied heavily on Marshall. As ambassador to China, Marshall attempted to negotiate an end to the Chinese civil war. Although he was unable to bring the war to a peaceful conclusion, he helped Truman resist pressure to send American troops to aid the Chinese Nationalists.

In 1947 he became Truman's secretary of state. In this position he was important in changing the American view of our role in the world. At a speech at Harvard on June 5, 1947, he proposed the massive postwar aid plan that later bore his name. The European Recovery Program, or "Marshall Plan," affirmed the United States' commitment in Europe and probably saved millions from starvation. In the first frantic days of the Berlin crisis, Truman was unsure how to respond to the Soviet blockade. Marshall led the cabinet members who rejected the use of force as a solution. The airlift was the alternative chosen.

Marshall resigned as secretary of state at the end of Truman's first term, and for a year was the president of the American Red Cross. After the Korean War broke out, in 1950, he returned to Truman's cabinet, serving as secretary of defense for the first year of the war. In 1951, after fifty years in public service, during which he had traveled 35,000 miles, he permanently retired.

In 1953 his efforts in the European Recovery Program were rewarded with a Nobel Peace Prize. Marshall was the first professional soldier to receive the award. He died on October 16, 1959. At his funeral, the usually reserved Harry Truman said, "He was the greatest general since Robert E. Lee. He was the man of honor, the man of truth, the man of greatest ability. He was the greatest of the great in our time."

The Marshall Foundation, founded after his death, plays an important role in maintaining the relationship between the United States and Western Europe. Every year, it sponsors young European leaders on tours of the United States. Prime Minister Margaret Thatcher of England and many other important Europeans have toured the United States as Marshall Fellows. The Marshall Plan helped to build American and European friendship into the relationship we enjoy today. It is appropriate that the foundation bears Marshall's name, as it carries on the work of sustaining that friendship.

the movement toward isolation reversed itself, and overseas aid became a major part of American foreign policy. The most important architect of this effort was George C. Marshall. As a general, Marshall had served as the U.S. Army Chief of Staff during the war and had become Truman's secretary of state after retiring from the military. On June 5, 1947, Marshall spoke at Harvard University, outlining the plan that would eventually bear his name. The Marshall Plan was a huge offer of American aid to the countries of war-ravaged Europe.

The first ship bearing Marshall Plan aid arrives at Bordeaux, France.

Marshall was careful to mention that no country was excluded from the offer. A country was eligible as long as it did not interfere with another country receiving aid. Marshall and some others thought that the Soviet Union was likely to reject the aid in its satellite countries as unwanted American influence. This would mean that the aid could go to the nations of Western Europe, which were struggling against Communist movements and the threat of the Soviet army.

Eleven days after Marshall's speech, the plan was attacked in the Soviet Communist Party newspaper *Pravda*, and two weeks later the Soviet Union forbade all countries under its control to participate. With American technology, money, and assistance going only to Western Europe, the division of the continent into American and Soviet spheres of influence was complete.

In July 1947 an article appeared in *Foreign Affairs* magazine. It was called "Sources of Soviet Conduct," and the name of the author was given only as "X." The writer was actually George F. Kennan, an official of the State Department who had served in the Soviet Union. He used the anonymous article to warn that the Soviet Union was hostile and aggressive, and that any agreements with its government were good only as long as the Kremlin found them useful. Kennan suggested a policy of "containment." By this he meant reacting to Soviet aggression wherever it arose, and thereby limiting the expansion of communism. This policy soon became the official United States strategy for dealing with the Soviet Union. It set the stage for a direct contest of superpowers in postwar Europe.

During this period Great Britain suffered worse shortages than in the days of the Nazi bombings. The people of France had seen their government change hands many times as different political parties suggested solutions to impossible problems. In the bitter winter of 1947–1948 it seemed that Europe had survived the war only to collapse during peace. The arrival of American aid, going to the victors as well as Italy, western Germany, and other nations, made the United States the most important force in the stability and survival of Western Europe. Coal for the winter, food for the hungry millions, and materials to rebuild the shattered cities of Europe began to arrive overseas. In two years $15 billion in aid reached Western Europe.

The Soviet Union saw the Marshall Plan as a threat to its security. The prospect of a rebuilt Germany frightened Stalin. He tightened his control over the Soviet-occupied Eastern European countries. He called for an organization of communist parties from different countries, the Cominform, which would allow him to control personally all the communist countries in Eastern Europe. In Czechoslovakia, the brief cooperation between Communists and other elected parties came to an end. In February of 1948 the Czech government moved toward accepting Marshall Plan aid. Communist members of the cabinet, under direction from Moscow, or-

Dean Acheson was Under-Secretary of State to President Truman. Secretary of State George Marshall, a military man, was inexperienced in foreign affairs and often relied on Acheson for guidance.

dered the police to arrest the other parties' leadership. After some bloodshed, democracy was abolished in Czechoslovakia, and the Soviet bloc in Eastern Europe was secure.

Truman reacted with an angry speech and asked Congress to resume the draft. The American army had shrunk to one-fifth the size of the Soviet army, but now it began to grow again. On that same day, March 17, 1948, representatives from France, Britain, Belgium, Luxembourg, and the Netherlands gathered to sign a treaty for their mutual defense. It was called the Brussels Treaty. The countries that signed the treaty claimed it was to protect against future threats from Germany. But Stalin knew that the treaty was in response to his aggressive policies.

As Europe divided into two opposing camps, the question of what to do with Germany became more important. The Allies had thought that the partition of Germany was only temporary. Now, however, a reunited Germany seemed impossible. The Americans had offered to unify their zone with the others. The Soviets had rejected the plan, but on December 2, 1946, the British had accepted. This British and American unity was the foundation of an independent West Germany, formed out of the zones occupied by the democratic Allies.

The next step was the creation of a West German currency. When the Western powers moved to introduce this

A Berliner works amid the rubble of his city. Behind him, a poster reads, "Berlin Emergency Program, with Marshall Plan Help."

long-needed reform, the Soviets protested. A new currency implied a new country, and the Soviet Union wanted Germany to remain divided, disordered, and in political limbo. The new Germany forming with Western encouragement was a threat. The city of Berlin, a Western outpost deep inside Soviet territory, was the heart of that threat. On March 20, 1947, the Soviets withdrew their representative from the Allied Control Council in Berlin. There were now two Berlins, one Soviet and the other controlled by the West.

In the days before the currency reform was made official, trains heading to Berlin through Soviet territory were stopped and searched. Delays on the western routes to the city became common, and blackouts reminded Berliners that the Soviets controlled the city's electrical generators. On June 18, 1948, the currency reform was officially announced.

Berliners were not surprised when almost all surface traffic into the city was stopped that night. The Soviets claimed that there were "technical difficulties," but Berliners knew it was the beginning of a siege. The Soviet Union had challenged the United States over the control of Europe, and the inhabitants of Berlin realized that their fate rested on the outcome.

3

"OPERATION VITTLES"

When news of the blockade first came from Berlin, the Allies were not sure how to respond. General Clay, in command of the American zone of Germany, immediately stopped all trade with the eastern zone. By June 24, 1948, when the power was cut off, he had already ordered cargoes of food to be airlifted into the city. Then Clay made a bold proposal. He wanted to send an army engineer company into Soviet territory with an offer to help with the "technical difficulties." If they were met with resistance, tanks would be sent to assist them. Clay believed that the Soviets, confronted with force, would back down. He realized that such a move would risk war with the Soviet Union, however, and waited for word from the president.

In Washington, opinion was divided. Many of Truman's advisers cautioned

Young Berliners atop a mountain of rubble cheer a C-54 "Skymaster" as it passes overhead.

him that Berlin was impossible to save. The six thousand Allied troops there were no match for the Soviet army, and none of the Western European nations was ready for war. Stalin had struck at American influence where it was weakest, on a tiny island of democracy far inside Soviet-occupied Europe.

Others in Truman's cabinet agreed with General Clay. They felt that force was necessary to end the threat to Berlin and the rest of Western Europe. If the United States retreated from Berlin, they argued, then other Europeans would question the resolve of the United States. Stalin would make more and more demands, gathering confidence in the face of American weakness, until it would be too late or too dangerous to make a stand.

Truman was caught between the specter of another war, so soon after the last one, and the prospect of letting Europe slip into Soviet hands without a fight. His first reaction was to proclaim

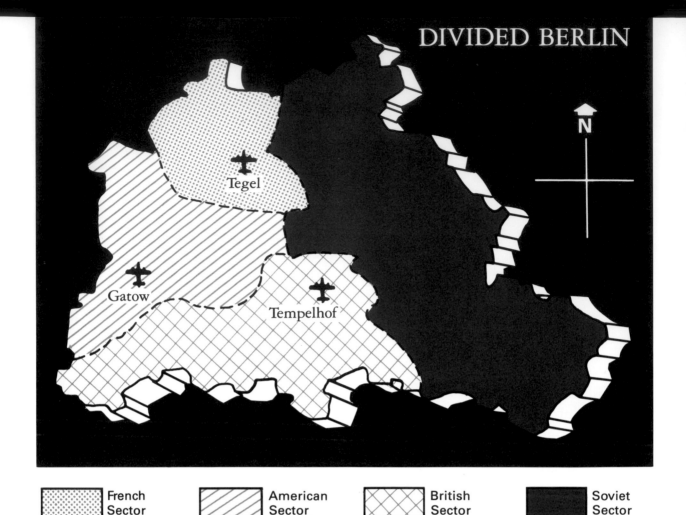

that the United States would remain in Berlin. "We are going to stay, period," he said. But he resisted Clay's suggestion that a display of force was the answer. The only option remaining was to continue with the airlift Clay had launched, and hope it could feed 2 million Berliners until another solution was found. The airlift was, at first, only a temporary measure, a way for Truman to avoid the terrible choice that Stalin had presented him.

The airlift, called "Operation Vittles" by the press, began as an improvisation, a collection of hastily assembled airplanes and crews. The first loads flown into the airports of western Berlin were only symbolic of American support. In 1948 most people had never flown in an aircraft. It was before the days when air transport and air travel were familiar around the globe. The notion that 2 million people could be fed by airlift was incredible. As the siege lengthened, General Clay realized that, incredible or not, the airlift would *have* to feed the citizens of Berlin.

He had one advantage in this effort. During the war, more aircraft had been built than in all the years before, and a large number of pilots had been trained to fly them. The huge cargo aircraft used in the war were now scattered all over the world, but as the airlift became a priority, they were recalled to Europe from Asia and the Americas. Many of the airlift crews included British pilots who had fought bravely in the Battle of Britain but who had returned to civilian life without hope of flying again. World War II had confirmed the importance of air power in war. Now the airlift demonstrated the importance of peacetime air transport, and these men found themselves taking to the air again.

The most overpowering problem for the airlift to overcome was the weight of sheer numbers. The 2 million besieged Berliners needed food, medicine, fuel, and all the other products usually taken for granted in a large city. The organizers set as their target 8 million pounds of supplies a day. This was barely enough to assure that Berliners got 1,800 calories per day each, and that hospitals and other essential services could get supplies and electricity.

The transport plane that was the most common in the Allied air forces was the C-47, also called the Dakota. This plane had served in the British Burma campaign, where troops deep in the jungle had been supplied almost completely by air. However, the Dakota could carry only 6,000 pounds of cargo. At that rate, more than a thousand flights a day would have to enter Berlin's two airports. A newer, unproven plane was the Douglas Skymaster (the C-54), which could carry three times as

The C-47 was the first plane to be equipped with its own elevator to assist loading and unloading.

much as the Dakota. The British Royal Air Force had recently converted one of its large bombers, the Lancaster, into a transport. The Lancaster could carry as much as a Skymaster, and was faster. These larger planes were essential to the airlift's success, since each of them could carry in one load the daily supplies for 5,000 Berliners.

Since the British and Americans were attempting something never done before, they ran into many problems that were new in the history of aviation. One difficulty was that Berlin needed an average of 30 tons of salt each day. The Allies had trouble finding containers to transport the salt. It leaked through bags and ate away metal drums, winding up on the floor of the cargo cabin. There, the corrosive salt could rust through the airplane's control wires. The Allies solved the problem by carrying the salt on sea planes, which were built to be exposed to the ocean's salt spray. These Sunderland "flying boats" had control wires in the roof rather than below the floorboards.

An even more troublesome cargo was coal. No matter what precautions were taken, coal dust seeped out of the containers, blackening plane and crew alike. Coal is also a very bulky substance, and it took up room needed for other supplies. As winter deepened, and more and more coal was required to heat the city, the Allies turned to liquid fuels, such as kerosene. Berliners converted their heaters to the new fuels while ground crews created tanker-aircraft to carry the dangerous, flammable liquids.

Another way that the Allies saved cargo space was by dehydrating, or drying out, food. Food with the water

The needs of the blockaded city made flights necessary twenty-four hour a day. This picture was taken by General Lucius Clay, architect of the airlift, himself.

An American plane crashes just inside Berlin. In all, seventy-nine American and British airmen were killed during the airlift.

taken out is much lighter. Dehydrated potatoes were an important part of besieged Berlin's diet, since they were one-fifth the weight of normal potatoes. Water was added to them once they had arrived in Berlin. Fortunately, the city had deep wells from which water could be drawn.

While the planners of the airlift made every effort to increase its efficiency, the men who flew and serviced the aircraft pushed themselves and their machines to the limit. A flight crew would make the one-hour flight to Berlin from western Germany, wait for an hour or less while the plane was unloaded, and then make the return flight as soon as possible. They repeated this routine two times a day. Often the flights would be made in bad weather, since the demand for coal and food grew as the winter months brought cold and snow. Some pilots found themselves landing on runways they could not see, given careful instructions from the radar-equipped ground controllers. These dangerous landings were made in the heart of a densely populated city, where one mistake might bring disaster. After aircraft began arriving from American bases around the world, a night shift was added, and the airports hummed with activity twenty-four hours a day. Yet of the 200,000 flights made during the lift, few ended in tragedy. In all, only seventy-nine British and American air-

37

men were killed during the operation.

One of the greatest limitations the Allies faced was a lack of airports. Although there were enough airports in the Allied-occupied zones of Germany, only two were in western Berlin itself at the airlift's beginning. One was Gatow, which had a concrete runway that the Royal Air Force was close to finishing. This was fortunate, because the huge four-engine planes essential to the airlift could use only a strong, modern runway. Once the blockade started, though, it was difficult to get building materials to complete the job. The British rose to the occasion, using, instead of concrete, the fragments of roads that had been bombed during the war. This was one of the many ironies of the airlift. The ruins of the city, which Allied bombers had almost destroyed, were being used to create a runway for those very Allied planes. This time, however, the converted Lancaster bombers were bringing not bombs but food, medicine, and fuel for the besieged city.

The American airport in Berlin was Templehof. It was near the center of town, and Berliners were constantly aware of the steady procession of airplanes passing close overhead. Since the two Berlin airports were the city's lifeline, the Allies kept them as busy as possible. At Gatow, a plane took off or landed every ninety seconds. Air traffic was so dense that a pilot who overshot his landing and had to pull away could not come back for a second pass. The plane behind him would already be coming in to land. Different types of aircraft were assigned different altitudes, with only a few minutes' clearance between an airplane and the craft behind it.

Even with the two airports operating at full capacity, the target of 8 million pounds of cargo a day was out of reach. The French and Americans decided to build a third airport in the French sector. It was called Tegel, and was built of materials airlifted into Berlin as well as whatever could be salvaged. Berliners themselves labored on this airport, and contributed their efforts to improve the other two. The workers were given special ration cards, without which the hard labor would have been impossible. Even with extra food, however, the Berliners' meager diet made the backbreaking work more difficult than ever. When Tegel was completed, they were rewarded with a new stream of airplanes landing in Berlin. The "temporary" airlift had stretched from June 1948 into the winter, with no end in sight. With the new airport, however, the quantity of supplies finally began to reach and even exceed the original target.

Although the survival of the city now seemed assured, there were still many hardships facing the citizens of Berlin. As winter fell, the temporary electrical generator the Allies had flown in a piece at a time was run less and less. It had supplied electricity during part of the day, but now the city's small supply of coal was needed for heating homes. In the coldest months, Berliners received only two hours of electricity a

"UNCLE WIGGLYWINGS"

Conditions in blockaded Berlin were very harsh. Germany had lost 3½ million soldiers in the war, and Berlin was a city of orphans and widows. The food rations were neither plentiful nor appealing. Dried potatoes, bread, powdered eggs, and cereal were the only "vittles" that many Berliners received day after day. As the months wore on, hunger and the dullness of the food took its toll on the children of the ruined city.

Alongside the airlift, American personnel involved in feeding the city began another, unofficial operation. "Operation Little Vittles," as it was called, delivered candy donated by Allied servicemen to the children of Berlin. It was started by Lieutenant Gale Anderson. He began bringing small loads of sweets with him on his cargo runs. As he passed over the heads of children gathered to watch the planes land, he would wiggle the wings of his aircraft. This was the signal to them that he was about to drop the candy. This earned him the name "Uncle Wigglywings."

The operation grew as more pilots became "candy-bombers." From Mobile, Alabama, where Lt. Anderson had been previously based, came 500 pounds of donated handkerchiefs. They were used to make parachutes for the candy drops. Many of the same pilots who had bombed the city four years earlier were now cheered as they passed overhead. Sweets had replaced the terrible weapons that had laid the city to waste.

Each day, many grateful Berliners watched the landings from the huge piles of rubble that dotted the landscape. Some greeted the aircraft in person and brought the fliers modest gifts from their few remaining possessions. The Allied airmen brought cigarettes or newspapers as souvenirs from the outside world. On the crowded runways, Americans and Germans exchanged these small presents. For the first time in a decade, they met not as enemies, nor as the victorious and the defeated, but as friends.

day. These two hours sometimes came in the middle of the night. Although the Berliners' food rations increased steadily, they were never very large.

In eastern Berlin, conditions were also affected by the blockade. Past the ring of Soviet checkpoints, the counterblockade imposed by the Western powers was further disrupting the fragile East German economy. Although eastern Berliners had a steady supply of electricity and better rations, the superpowers' struggle was felt throughout the divided country.

Another fact influenced life in blockaded Berlin. Food and heat are necessary for survival, but everyone also depends on small luxuries that they take for granted most of the time. The Allies realized this, and flew in coffee, newspapers, and sometimes even cigars. Of course, the supply of these "luxuries" never met the demand for them. Soon, the black market became an important part of every Berliner's existence. Allied air crews would carry a carton of chocolates or cigarettes with their loads, bringing a high price from the city's inhabitants. Profit-minded Soviet officers, who could pass through the checkpoints without being searched, smuggled in luxuries from the Eastern bloc.

The embassies of other Eastern European countries were important sources of the goods that could not officially be obtained. Their diplomatic immunity protected them from searches by the blockade's enforcers. Stores in the eastern sector, tolerated by the Soviets, sold luxuries to western Berliners.

In many ways, the blockade was imperfect, reflecting the hesitation of the Soviets to completely choke the city. The Soviets continued to supply Gatow airport with electricity, even when the rest of the city had been cut off. West Berliners were even allowed to sign up for ration cards in the eastern sector. Few did so, however, because to the proud Berliners relying on the Soviets seemed like surrender.

The airlift was a very cautious and strange encounter. Soviet fighter planes could have shot down the lumbering cargo aircraft, just as Soviet troops could have swept through Berlin's military defenses, but they did not. The Americans resisted the temptation to settle the matter by force, even though General Clay was convinced that the Soviets would back down. The airlift was unlike the merciless conflict of World War II, where whole cities had been destroyed. Instead, the two sides were reluctant to pursue the contest as an all-out battle, preferring solutions that left their opponent peaceful options. The airlift was just such a solution. Truman had supported it rather than face the terrible prospect of war.

The reason for this caution was that both the United States and the U.S.S.R. felt threatened by the other's military advantages. The United States feared the huge Soviet army, which could have advanced through Western Europe almost without resistance. The fragile democracies the United States had given so much to support would have toppled in an instant. On the other hand, the

Soviet Union feared the United States' nuclear monopoly. The United States had developed the atomic bomb in World War II and had used it against the Japanese, but the Soviet Union had not yet produced its own nuclear weapons. Thus, the two sides seemed paralyzed. Neither was willing to make a bold move that would force the other to respond boldly in return. So the Berlin encounter resembled a negotiation rather than a war, the contenders each seeking an advantage but resisting the temptation to push their opponent too hard.

The United States triumphed in the encounter. Truman recognized that the Soviets controlled the land routes leading to Berlin. Rather than force the issue, the United States found another way to supply the city. The Soviets, thinking that the airlift would fail, permitted the transports to fly over Soviet territory. With the airlift's success, world opinion turned against the Soviets. The sight of their armies attempting to starve 2 million civilians while the Americans and British bravely worked to feed them was a disaster for Soviet propaganda.

As winter ended, the weather cleared and the cargo tonnage steadily increased. With all three airports working at capacity, the supplies entering the city reached the level where they had been before the blockade. Although the airlift was still expensive and inconvenient, there was no doubt that the city had been saved. In eastern Germany, the West's trade embargo was proving effective. The eastern zone had been

As news of the airlift's end spreads, Berliners rally at Schoeneberger city hall to celebrate.

ravaged after the war by the Soviet policy of taking everything of value. Being cut off from the West during the blockade only made matters worse for the struggling eastern Germans. West Germany, on the other hand, was completing its constitutional convention, and the new country was on the verge of being officially formed. As early as January 1949, Stalin stated in an interview that the blockade might be discontinued if the West's embargo was also raised.

As the blockade faltered, Western Europe was on the verge of formally uniting in mutual defense. The five members of the Brussels Treaty had joined in negotiations with Canada,

On the White House lawn, President Truman presents General Lucius Clay with a medal for his work in the Berlin airlift.

Denmark, Iceland, Italy, Norway, Portugal, and the United States. The new group was called the North Atlantic Treaty Organization, or NATO. President Truman signed the treaty on April 2, 1949, committing the United States to the defense of all of Western Europe. Eleven European nations were now united against threats to their security.

In March 1949 several of the Soviet officials in charge of the blockade were recalled to Moscow. There were talks concerning Berlin at the United Nations throughout April. The Soviets asked that in exchange for lifting the blockade, the formation of West Germany be postponed. The United States and Britain refused. On May 4 an agreement was reached. No concessions were made to the Soviets apart from raising the em-

bargo of Eastern Europe. On May 12, 1949, the blockade was lifted. The exhausted Berliners celebrated throughout the city when the news was released. Allied flyers set a record of 1,017 flights on this final day. The Allies had made a total of 200,000 flights, and delivered more than 1 1/2 million *tons* of supplies, at a cost of $5 million per day. The blockade had lasted 318 days. On the very day it was lifted, the occupying powers approved the new West German constitution. The elected Parliamentary Council had adopted the document on May 8, the fourth anniversary of the war's end. The long siege was over, but even as the barriers between East and West Berlin were lowered, the division of Germany and Europe was more complete than ever.

ICELAND
1949

Atlantic Ocean

NORWAY
1949

SWEDEN

FINLAND

U.S.S.R.

DENMARK
1949

North Sea

Baltic Sea

IRELAND

GREAT
BRITAIN
1949

NETHER-
LANDS
1949

Berlin

EAST
GER-
MANY

POLAND

Warsaw Pact Formed 1955

BELGUIM
1949

WEST
GER-
MANY
1955

CZECHOSLOVAKIA

LUX.
1949

FRANCE
1949-1966

SWITZ.

AUSTRIA

HUNGARY

ROMANIA

Black Sea

ITALY
1949

YUGOSLAVIA

BULGARIA

SPAIN
1982

ALBA-
NIA
- 1968

GREECE
1952

TURKEY
1952

Mediterranean Sea

DIVIDED EUROPE

| | NATO | | Nonaligned or Neutral | | Warsaw Pact |

43

4

THE WALL

The early morning quiet of August 13, 1961, was shattered by the roar of trucks and armored troop carriers moving through East Berlin. They unloaded men and equipment at the borders of the Western sectors. Without warning, West Berlin was surrounded by an army of 50,000 East German workers, police, and soldiers. In the darkness before dawn, there was frantic activity all along the line that separated the Eastern and Western sectors of Berlin. By sunrise, the workers had erected a barrier of barbed wire and fences between the two parts of the city. Subway and train service across the barrier was halted. The frontier between East and West in the divided city had been closed.

West Berliners awoke to a city suddenly split in two. Families and church congregations had been divided. Work-

President John F. Kennedy visits Berlin in 1963. Here, he mounts a viewing stand to see East Berlin across the wall.

ers were cut off from their jobs. Next-door neighbors found themselves separated from each other by an impassable barrier.

This time, however, it was not West Berlin that was being blockaded. Neither the city's electricity nor its ground links with West Germany were cut off. This time, the Soviets had moved against the people of East Berlin. The barrier was put in place to prevent East Germans from escaping to the West through the gateway of divided Berlin. The free passage to West Germany that Berlin represented was now blocked. Ten days after the first barrier appeared, the East Germans constructed a wall along the sector boundary. When the wall was finished, the political division of Berlin, and of Germany and Europe, had been cast in stone.

The unrest that had finally forced the East German government to imprison its people had been building since the end of World War II. Walter Ulbricht, an

East German Communist who had lived in the Soviet Union during World War II, had been installed as the head of the Communist Party when the Soviets occupied eastern Germany. The Ulbricht government was left with an economy that the Soviets had deliberately destroyed. During the 1948 blockade of western Berlin the Allies cut off trade with the Soviet zone. This further slowed recovery efforts and made East Germans angry at the Soviets.

After ruling for almost three decades, Joseph Stalin had become the living symbol of Soviet oppression. His death, on March 5, 1953, awakened hopes that the Soviet Union's grip on Eastern Europe might relax. After a power struggle within the highest circles of the Communist Party, Nikita Khrushchev and Nikolai Bulganin emerged as Stalin's successors. Their willingness to maintain control of East Germany was soon tested.

Three months after Stalin's death, workers in East Berlin staged an unplanned strike. Several thousand workers, angered by long hours and low pay, their tempers frayed by the hot summer, suddenly ceased work and marched on government buildings. News of the strike spread, and early the next morning, June 17, 1953, more than 100,000 people filled the streets of the Soviet sector. The East German police were ruthless, firing freely on the crowd with machine guns. Soviet tanks were used to clear the streets, but the Soviets showed more restraint than the East German authorities. The rioters became more violent. They began burning buildings, and for a short time it seemed that a revolution was under way. The government called on the Soviet Union for help. The Soviets responded with more tanks and troops. Martial law was declared, and by the end of the day East Berlin was under the control of the Soviet army.

The strike spread to other East German cities, but the rioters were no match for Soviet tanks. Food was withheld from the strikers, and the Ulbricht government began a series of mass arrests. After a few tense days people started to return to work, and the violence was over. Stability had been restored for the moment, but the anger of the East German people still smoldered.

In the years from 1953 to 1961, many East Germans decided to escape the harsh conditions in the Soviet-run zone. East Berliners especially were aware of the growing prosperity in the Western-occupied area, since they could take a short walk and see it for themselves. The new West German state had been helped by Marshall Plan aid and by the manufacturing capacity of the Western-occupied Ruhr district. An East German who could get to East Berlin was only a subway ride away from freedom and prosperity.

Between 1950 and 1961, 4 million East Germans escaped from the Soviet bloc this way. These refugees were doctors, policemen, teachers, and other professionals who were essential to the recovery of East Germany. They totaled one-fourth of the country's population, and their flight threatened to wreck the structure of East German society. In 1958 Khrushchev grew frustrated with the lack of an agreement on the question of Germany. Although East and West Germany were separate nations by this time, the Soviet Union officially considered them one country. Khrushchev announced on November 10, 1958, that if a settlement was not reached in six months, the Soviet Union would sign a separate peace treaty with East Germany. This treaty would end all agreements between the Allies and the Soviet Union about Berlin. The implication was that the Allies' access to the city would be cut off.

The West was concerned about the new Soviet leader's threats. The memory of Soviet tanks in the 1953 East Berlin riots was fresh in President Dwight Eisenhower's mind. In 1956, during a popular uprising in Soviet-ruled Hungary, Khrushchev had proved again that he was willing to use force. In Hungary as in East Germany, the riots were crushed by a display of armored might.

President Eisenhower met with Premier Khrushchev in Paris, but without results. The conference was marred by the U-2 incident, in which an American spy plane had been shot down over the Soviet Union. Khrushchev used the violation of Soviet air space as an excuse to

A statue of Stalin lies toppled during the Hungarian uprising in 1956.

disrupt the meeting, and the negotiations fell short of a settlement. Khrushchev's time limit arrived and was extended, and the crisis eventually blew over.

Khrushchev raised the question of Berlin again in 1961. At a meeting with the new president, John F. Kennedy, on June 4, in Vienna, he again pronounced a six-month limit on the reunification of Germany. If this deadline was not met, the Soviet Union would consider East Germany an independent country, with total control over its capital city, Berlin. Kennedy responded by increasing the size of the United States army. He called up reserves and requested emergency money from Congress. Part of this money was for civil defense. Since Berlin could not be protected by NATO's outnumbered ground forces, Kennedy was preparing for the worst.

By August 1961 the flow of East Germans fleeing to West Germany had reached 1,500 escapees a day. The Soviets, through the East German government, finally moved to stop this dangerous loss of human resources. Khrushchev realized that any military attempt to capture Berlin would risk war, so he settled the division of Germany in a way that would keep the Ulbricht government from collapsing. The wall was the answer to the question of a divided Germany.

The first days after the barrier was built were tense ones. West Berliners protested near the Brandenburg Gate, under the suspicious watch of armed East German and Soviet guards. More than once American and British military police stepped in to prevent violence. Some buildings in East Berlin had windows that opened out over the western sector. People trapped in East Berlin by the barrier jumped from these windows to escape. Many were injured by the fall, and some were killed. East Germans also escaped by crashing through the wire in vehicles or running the few dangerous yards to safety. They were shot at by East German soldiers, and West Berlin police returned the fire. In those first days, at least a dozen escapees, police, and soldiers were killed. After the wall was built, and gradually reinforced, the escapes became fewer.

The human tragedy of the wall was most evident in the first few years of its existence. Couples with children brought them to the wall, so that relatives on the other side could see them at a distance. Marriage parties visited the wall, and waved to watching friends in East Berlin. Eventually, the East German authorities constructed blinds, so that people could no longer see across. The wall was built higher and higher in the years to come.

The cruelty of the wall is that it separates Germans from Germans. The East German border guards along the wall face fellow Germans across the barrier.

The Brandenburg Gate, a checkpoint between the eastern and western sectors, bristles with barbed wire a few days after work on the barrier had begun.

TO CROSS THE WALL

When the Berlin Wall was first constructed, it served only to reinforce the original barbed-wire barrier. The wall was one foot thick and five feet high. In those early days, many East Germans escaped in heavy trucks, crashing to freedom through the brick and barbed wire. Over the years, the wall has been strengthened and heightened several times. Escapees have had to show more and more ingenuity as the East German government improves the wall.

In 1963 eight people escaped by hiding themselves in a cable drum that was transported across the West German frontier. One of them, a seventeen-year-old girl, was forced to return to East Germany. Her parents, who had remained behind, had been threatened by the state security service. In 1964 a 150-yard-long tunnel was constructed by thirty-six students. It stretched from the cellar of a bakery in East Berlin to an exit perilously close to a Soviet checkpoint. The builders had carefully calculated the length and direction of the tunnel so that it emerged just inside the Western sector. In all, fifty-seven people escaped.

The wall has often been the scene of violence. Almost a hundred East Germans are known to have been killed while attempting to escape. West German police have often fired warning shots or tear gas to distract or threaten East German border guards in pursuit of escapees. Eight East German guards have been killed in these clashes. In 1964 twenty-year-old Hans Meyer had made it through the barbed-wire fences, but was shot just as he reached the wall. When East Germans arrived to carry him back, an American soldier named Hans Pool climbed up from the western side and boldly challenged them. When West Berlin police fired warning shots, Meyer was released.

The last round of construction in 1976 left the wall almost six feet thick, wider than its original height. It stands 13 feet tall and is buffered by a 100-yard-wide zone of guard towers, vicious dogs, and concrete barriers. Electronic sensors and floodlights complete the barrier and have made escape over the wall almost impossible. Many East Germans continue to escape from Soviet-occupied Europe, but most flee through other countries or across the wider East-West German border. An estimated 5,000 East Germans a year escape through other avenues.

In addition to these dramatic escapes, over 300,000 East Germans have emigrated to the West legally since 1961. Another 60,000 have been arrested for the crime of "attempting to flee the republic." Many of them are still in prison. The wall may have prevented the wholesale flight of the East German people, but it has not completely stopped the flight to freedom. In Berlin, the wall has made escape almost impossible. But as it runs through the streets and buildings of a great city, it stands as a glaring indictment of the Soviet system.

An East German soldier leaps to freedom a few hours after the barbed-wire barrier was erected.

They are required to shoot anyone who attempts to escape. In the first five years after the wall's construction, 2,000 East German soldiers and officers escaped themselves. One escaped border guard, Dieter Jentzen, wrote in defense of his fellow guards. "The number of those captured at the wall and shot would be at least ten times as high, if those serving there were merely carrying out orders. I call upon everyone in West Berlin to see through the uniform. See beyond those in power and establish an alliance from person to person. This alliance is what Ulbricht fears more than tanks."

Although the West was outraged by the inhumanity the wall represented, the situation in 1961 was puzzling. Since the Soviets had moved not against West Berlin but against the citizens of East Germany, it was difficult to respond forcefully. President John F. Kennedy sent General Lucius Clay to West Berlin as his ambassador. Clay, the architect of the airlift, was a welcome symbol of support, but it was unclear what he could do to help. The Allies considered tearing down the barbed-wire barrier, but the East Germans might have simply put it up again, farther inside their own sector. If they had, the Allies would have had to violate Soviet-controlled territory and risk war to tear it down again. Berlin was a hole in the iron curtain that the Soviets were determined to repair. Just as the United States could not permit the loss of Berlin in the earlier crisis, the Soviets could not allow the new East German state to drain away through this hole. Once

President Kennedy rides in a motorcade with Willy Brandt, Mayor of West Berlin and Konrad Adenauer, Chancellor of West Germany.

again, each side was careful not to force the other to overreact. The specter of nuclear war kept the opponents from direct confrontation.

If the United States had prevented the Soviets from closing the gateway of Berlin, it might have forced them to try to capture Berlin itself. The city was still isolated, and the Soviet army still far outnumbered NATO forces. The Allies could make only symbolic gestures. American tanks arrived and were greeted by cheering crowds. Although they were only token reinforcements, they showed that the city would not be abandoned by the West. British military police strung a barbed-wire barrier of their own around a monument to Rus-

sian war dead in West Berlin. They claimed it was to protect the monument from angry Berliners. The message of protest was clear.

Finally, President Kennedy himself went to West Berlin. On June 26, 1963, half a million people turned out to hear him speak. In his address he said, "All free men, wherever they may live, are citizens of Berlin." He ended his speech with the words *"Ich bin ein Berliner!"* "I am a Berliner!"

Berlin had become the front line of the conflict between East and West. The bravery of Berliners, in their threatened and isolated city, was cheered throughout the free world. The resistance to Soviet pressure in Berlin became a symbol for the rejection of tyranny everywhere, just as the wall has become symbolic of the miseries of Communist rule.

Twenty years earlier, Berlin had been Hitler's capital. Now, encircled by the wall, the city was viewed by the world as a citadel of freedom. The cold war, which had made enemies of the World War II Allies, had also made allies of bitter enemies. Great Britain, France, and the United States found themselves pro-tecting at any cost the Germany they had fought in the world war.

The wall made the situation in Berlin more stable. Although tensions ran high at first, the Allies eventually accepted this new division of Berlin. By preventing East Germany's collapse the wall may have deterred a nuclear war. For East and West Germans alike, however, the human cost of this solution was high indeed.

Many artists have used the western side of the wall as a canvas, to brighten its grim face or protest its existence. This 200-yard stretch of wall was painted by American artist Keith Haring.

AFTERWORD

TOWARD DÉTENTE, SLOWLY

On September 1, 1949, two American seaplanes were flying over western Alaska, only a few miles from the easternmost tip of the Soviet Union. They were equipped with Geiger counters, devices that detect radiation in the air. During their mission, the Geiger counters began to chatter. The flight crews recorded levels of radiation that could only be the result of an atomic explosion in the Soviet Union. The U.S.S.R. had become a nuclear power.

In the United States, the reaction to the discovery was one of shock and dismay. American scientists had assumed that it would take the Soviets several more years to develop an A-bomb. The security of Western Europe was thought to rest on the American monopoly of nuclear arms. If the Soviets now had the bomb, what would stop them from using their crushing advantage in con-

President Dwight D. Eisenhower reviews troops in Korea. He made the trip shortly after his election, fulfilling a campaign promise.

ventional forces? Since the Berlin blockade had turned the wartime allies against each other, Americans had felt that Soviet aggression had been restrained by the bomb. When the news of a Soviet nuclear detonation became public, Americans realized that the cold war had entered a new phase.

The United States and the Soviet Union faced each other in the center of Europe, but their conflict touched every part of the globe. Only in Berlin were American and Soviet ground forces actually at risk of clashing, but elsewhere the struggle between democracy and communism often brought the world close to another global war. In many small countries the United States and the Soviet Union supported opposing sides in smaller conflicts, called "brush-fire wars." Military assistance to friendly forces, which was sometimes secret, became an important factor in American and Soviet foreign policy. Cold war conflicts were carried out in small countries rather than across the borders of divided Europe. These smaller struggles held less risk of igniting a nuclear war.

The first major clash of the nuclear era came late in Harry Truman's presidency, less than a decade after World War II had ended. The conflict occurred halfway around the world from Berlin, on the Korean peninsula in East Asia. Korea had been occupied by the Japanese from 1910 until the end of World War II. In 1945, Korea, like Berlin, was divided between the Soviet Union and the United States. The southern part of the peninsula was under American control. The northern half was ruled by a Communist government. The peninsula was meant to be reunited after a brief period. This hopeful promise, like so many others in the postwar world, was never fulfilled.

To the north of this divided peninsula was China, led by Communist Party Chairman Mao Zedong (Mao Tsetung). The Communists had gained power in China in 1949, defeating the American-supported Chinese Nationalists. The Nationalists retreated to the island of Taiwan and were recognized as the sole government of China by the United States until 1972. Mao's China (the People's Republic of China) on the Asian mainland was allied with Moscow but independent of Stalin's direct control.

On June 25, 1950, the North Korean army, which had been trained in the Soviet Union, invaded South Korea. The Communists achieved complete surprise, and South Korean forces soon collapsed. Washington realized that if help were not sent immediately, Korea would be unified on Moscow's terms. The United Nations met in an emergency session, but the Soviet ambassador was absent. The Soviet Union had decided to boycott the Security Council because Communist China was not represented on it. Without the Soviets to halt it with a veto, a resolution was passed and UN forces were committed to assist the South Koreans. Troops were soon deployed under the UN flag, although the majority of them were American.

By September 1950 the South Korean army and the first American troops had retreated to the end of the peninsula, where they readied for a final stand. On September 15 General Douglas MacArthur, commander of the U.S. ground forces, made a desperate gamble, landing his forces behind enemy lines at Inchon, Korea. In twelve days he had recaptured Seoul, the South Korean capital, and cut off the supplies of the overextended Communists. Suddenly, the situation was reversed. The North Koreans were in retreat, and the American-led United Nations force was poised to take the Korean peninsula.

On September 30, 1950, the Chinese warned that they would enter the war if American forces crossed into North Korea. Seven days later General MacArthur ignored this warning. On November 26 the Chinese forces attacked, and again American troops were in flight.

After months of hard fighting, the

An American rocket launcher is used by UN forces in Korea.

Chinese offensive also ground to a halt. By the summer of 1951 the line between North and South Korea was almost exactly where it had started. After two more years of inconclusive struggle, a cease-fire was signed on July 27, 1953. The war had cost more than 50,000 American lives and risked a nuclear exchange, but in the end the map of East Asia had not been changed. An important effect of the war was to strengthen the determination of NATO. The organization's members now realized that the Soviet Union, which had helped spark the conflict, was ready to wage war to increase its empire.

The war against communism in Korea created a climate of suspicion at home. On Febuary 9, 1950, Wisconsin Senator Joseph McCarthy made a speech claiming that he had a list of 205 State Department officials who were Communist spies. This was the beginning of McCarthy's crusade to root out a gigantic "Communist conspiracy" that he claimed threatened the United States from within.

McCarthyism, as it came to be known, became an epidemic that touched every part of American life. The accusations made in Washington were echoed at local levels across the country. Teachers, entertainers, writers, and businessmen all found themselves accused of Communist sympathies with little proof. Though there was no evidence against them, these people often found themselves unemployed and shunned.

It was not until Dwight Eisenhower's presidency that McCarthy, at the height of his power, went too far in his accusations. In 1953 he attacked the United States army. In televised hearings, he harassed decorated generals and patriotic young enlisted men, and earned the anger of President Eisenhower, who had commanded the Allied armed forces in World War II. On December 2, 1954, the Senate voted to censure McCarthy for his conduct, and his power was broken.

America's fear of communism in the early cold war caused many mistakes to be made. By John F. Kennedy's presidency, McCarthyism had ended, but fear of communism still played an important role in American politics. The young president hoped to strike a blow against communism with an invasion of Cuba. The invasion was meant to topple the regime of Fidel Castro, a Cuban revolutionary who had seized power in his country and then allied it with the So-Soviet Union. Fifteen hundred Cubans who had escaped to the United States after Castro's revolution were trained by the U.S. Central Intelligence Agency as a secret anti-Castro military force. With American help, these exiles hoped to spark a new revolution by invading Cuba at the Bahía de Cochinos, or the Bay of Pigs.

Preparations for the operation had started during Eisenhower's presidency, and Kennedy decided to carry out the plan. The tiny force was caught on the beaches by Castro's army, and almost all were killed or captured. President Kennedy was embarrassed at home and abroad, and relations between Cuba and the United States have never returned to normal.

After the attempted invasion, the Soviets offered Castro arms to defend Cuba against a future American attack. The Soviet presence in Cuba grew and became more dangerous. In October 1962, with the situation in Berlin still tense after the building of the wall, President Kennedy learned just how dangerous it was. American surveillance flights over Cuba discovered newly installed Soviet nuclear missiles. Kennedy ordered the U.S. Navy to blockade Cuba and search any ships heading for Cuban ports. He demanded that Khrushchev remove the missiles. A dangerous contest of nerves began. Soviet freighters, escorted by a submarine, sailed to the edge of the blockaded zone. American warships and the Soviet submarine faced each other, their crews ready to fire the first shots of World War III. In Washington preparations were made for evacuation in case of a nuclear attack.

After a few tense hours, the Soviet ships retreated. Two days later, Khrushchev agreed to remove the missiles, in exchange for a guarantee that the United States would never invade Cuba. Kennedy also promised to dismantle a number of obsolete missiles at American bases in Turkey and Italy. In this confrontation, as in the others of the cold war, the situation remained the same after the two sides had come close to war. Neither could afford to press the other too hard, because the possibility of nuclear war demanded that conflicts be resolved by compromise.

The Cuban missile crisis was the closest the superpowers ever came to global destruction. Since that event, American and Soviet forces have not been in real danger of engaging in a battle. Both Soviet and American forces have . intervened in small countries, however, sometimes against opponents armed by the other superpower.

From 1965 to 1973 the United States committed hundreds of thousands of soldiers to protect South Vietnam. The Communist North Vietnamese army troops and Viet Cong guerrillas, who were supported by the U.S.S.R., were attempting to topple the government in the south. Here, American intervention failed, and the U.S. forces were withdrawn after mounting American casualties and opposition to the war at home made continuing the war impossible.

The Soviet Union also experienced the limits of its power when it invaded Afghanistan in December 1979. The pro-Soviet government there had been overthrown, and the Soviet military moved into the country to restore it to power. The United States openly shipped arms to rebels fighting the new Soviet-installed government. Ultimately, the Soviets withdrew their troops, beginning in 1988.

The allies of the two superpowers have often fought each other. In the Middle East, the United States has supported Israel in several wars, while Israel's hostile Arab neighbors receive arms from the Soviet Union. The United States has sent weapons to the anti-Communist *contra* rebels in Nicaragua, a Central American country that is friendly with the Soviet Union. Divided countries such as Angola and El Salvador have factions that are battling each other with help from the two superpowers. In these conflicts, the risk of war between the United States and Soviet Union is small, as long as the superpowers do not commit their own forces.

Many countries have tried to stay out of the East-West contest. Countries such as Egypt and India have accepted aid first from one superpower and then from the other. Nations like Iran have resisted moving toward either side. These "nonaligned nations" have grown in number since the early days of the cold war. Another important change in the map of the cold war is the break between Communist China and the Soviet Union. In the 1950s and 1960s, border disputes and political disagreements between the two countries led them to pursue different policies. Today there are really three superpowers.

President Richard Nixon made an unprecedented visit to the People's Republic of China to open relations with that Communist country. He is shown here on the Great Wall of China.

China has often been friendlier with the United States than it has with the Soviet Union.

Even though the Soviet Union and the United States have struggled against each other indirectly, relations between the two have grown friendlier and more stable. After the Cuban missile crisis, the two governments realized the importance of quick communication in times of tension. A direct phone connection, called the "Hot Line," was installed so that the American president and the Soviet general secretary could speak directly to each other at any time.

Negotiations between the two countries have resulted in treaties that limit the number of nuclear weapons maintained by each side. In 1972 President Richard Nixon made a historic visit to the People's Republic of China, opening diplomatic relations with that Communist country for the first time. In that same year, the Strategic Arms Limitation Talks produced a treaty called SALT I. It was followed in 1979, under President Jimmy Carter, by the SALT II treaty, which, although never ratified by the Senate, has since been observed by both sides.

This spirit of cooperation between the two superpowers is often called détente, from the French word for "relaxation." Events like the Soviet invasion of Afghanistan disturb détente, but relations have generally improved over the years. The Soviets have become important trading partners, and in 1976 the space programs of the two countries staged a joint effort called the Apollo-Soyuz mission.

In 1983 a new leader, Mikhail Gorbachev, rose to power in the Soviet Union. He represents a new generation of Soviet leadership, and his calls for an opening of his society and friendlier relations with the West have improved détente. A treaty removing all medium-range missiles from Europe, signed by Gorbachev and President Ronald Reagan in December 1987, is one result of better relations. It was the first treaty to actually reduce the number of nuclear weapons in the superpower arsenals. Although relations between the two countries seem better than they have been since World War II, it is impossible to tell whether the thaw in the cold war will last. There are still many differences between the United States and the Soviet Union. In Berlin the wall still divides a great European city, and the border between East and West Germany is still lined with troops and tanks.

Not one of the weary statesmen of World War II thought that this frontier would divide Europe for forty years, but a generation of Germans on both sides have grown up separated from their fellow Germans. As long as the wall stands, the fundamental difference between the two superpowers is cast in stone. The wall is a reminder that the occupied peoples of Eastern Europe are imprisoned. The freedom represented by West Berlin is a threat to the Soviet system of oppression and intimidation. The prosperity of the western sector is a reminder of the failed economic promises of communism.

West Berliners must also live with the wall. No part of their surrounded city is far from the watchtowers just across the sector boundary. The grim

A 1975 joint U.S.-Soviet space mission is commemorated on this set of American postage stamps.

President Ronald Reagan and Mikhail Gorbachev confer in Washington, DC, in December 1987. Eventually, the two negotiated the Intermediate Nuclear Forces Treaty,

This memorial at Templehof airport commemorates the seventy-nine airmen killed during the airlift.

face of the wall confronts them from every direction. The threat of Soviet aggression still hangs over the city, and French, American, and British forces still patrol the closed frontier. The barbed wire along the boundary is so long it could be stretched around the world, and the division it represents has indeed become global.

In a sense, we all live in the shadow of the wall. Berlin, a divided city, is a powerful symbol for our divided world. But even in its precarious situation, the city has survived crisis after crisis. The cold war has flared up many times, but so far it has not become a world war. Even in Berlin, where Soviet and American troops stand face to face, both sides have shown restraint, and proved that war can be avoided. So Berlin is also a hopeful symbol. In crisis and hardship, Berliners have shown courage and resolve. Perhaps in their story lies the greatest hope that the fragile peace will be maintained.

INDEX

Page numbers in *italics* indicate illustrations

SUGGESTED READING

CLAY, LUCIUS. *Decision in Germany*. New York: Doubleday, 1950.

HALLE, LOUIS J. *The Cold War as History*. New York: Harper & Row, 1967.

MORRIS, ERIC. *Blockade: Berlin and the Cold War*. New York: Stein and Day, 1973.

TRUMAN, HARRY S. *Year of Decisions*. New York: Doubleday, 1955.

DATE DUE

FOLLETT